Marygrove

EX LIBRIS

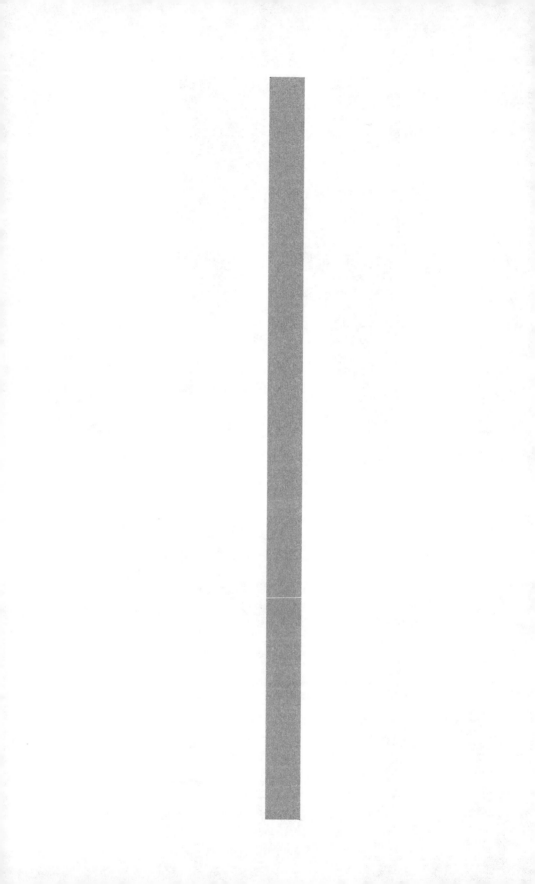

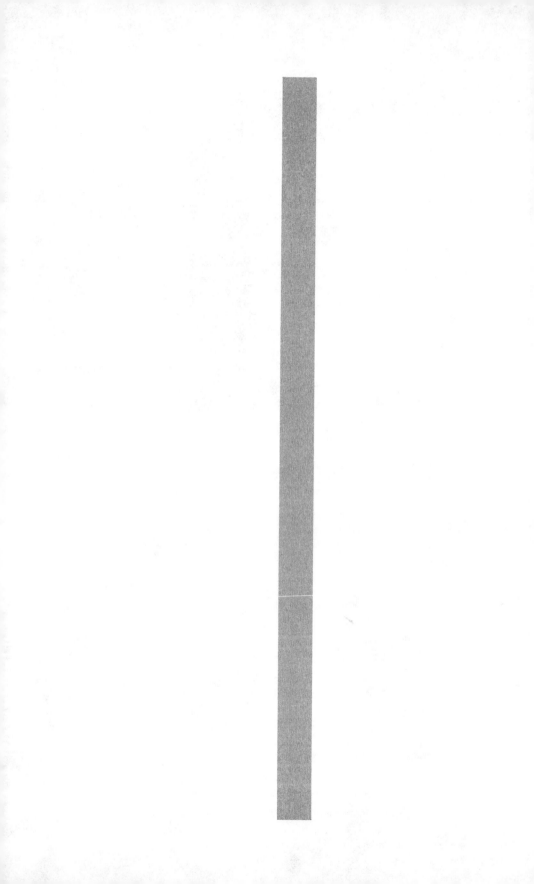

OEDIPUS AND JOB IN
WEST AFRICAN
RELIGION

OEDIPUS AND JOB IN WEST AFRICAN RELIGION

BY

MEYER FORTES

William Wyse Professor of Social Anthropology
in the University of Cambridge
Fellow of King's College

ι

CAMBRIDGE
AT THE UNIVERSITY PRESS
1959

PUBLISHED BY
THE SYNDICS OF THE CAMBRIDGE UNIVERSITY PRESS
Bentley House, 200 Euston Road, London, N.W. 1
American Branch: 32 East 57th Street, New York 22, N.Y.

©

CAMBRIDGE UNIVERSITY PRESS
1959

Printed in Great Britain at the University Press, Cambridge
(Brooke Crutchley, University Printer)

CONTENTS

CHAPTER I

FRAZER ON FATE

IT has been said that poets can be divided into two
classes. There are those who write for other
poets; and there are those who write for the
common reader. Anthropologists can be similarly
classified. There are the purists by conviction or by
habit who write only for their professional peers, and
there are the anthropologists of the forum and the
market-place who address themselves to the world
at large. But there are also a few who seem equally
at home in both worlds; and among these Sir James
Frazer was and remains without rival. His influence
on the progressive thought of his time is a by-word,
and his writings are still held in respect bordering
on awe outside professional anthropological circles.
Why then has his influence among his professional
successors declined in recent years? Chiefly, I think,
because he was not only a great anthropologist and
a man of letters, but also a moralist whose zeal in
spreading enlightenment too often got the better of
his scholarly judgement. That glittering prose hides
too many rash conjectures. The hypotheses paraded
with so much learning turn out to be little more
than descriptive labels for customs and institutions;

and the historical and psychological speculations used to eke them out seem naïve today. The smug contempt for the exotic beliefs and customs paraded with such gusto, and contrasted disparagingly with the 'civilized mind', repels us. Modern anthropology has largely grown away from Frazer; or rather it has outgrown him.

Yet, sooner or later, every serious anthropologist returns to the great Frazerian *corpus*. For beneath the encrustations of theory, speculation, and prejudice due to the climate of thought in which Frazer lived, there is a vision of mankind which still offers inspiration. It is a vision that takes in the whole of mankind. There lies its greatness. It shows in assiduous detail how varied and diverse are the customs and institutions of mankind. But its purpose is to bring home to us the unity behind the diversity. For Frazer this lay in supposed historical connexions or common mental habits and dispositions. Fallacious though his theories now prove to be, in principle he was right. There are uniformities and common patterns in the customs and institutions of mankind; and if we want to understand them we must take into account the common intellectual and emotional dispositions of mankind.

It would not have seemed strange to Frazer to place side by side Oedipus, Job and the religious beliefs of a West African tribe of ancestor worshippers, as I propose to do. But what he was interested in when he lumped together, as he habitually did, the customs of the Greeks and the Hebrews, other peoples of antiquity and contemporary primitive and Oriental societies, was their most superficial descriptive features. To take an instance at random, Orestes the matricide, recovering sanity by biting off a finger, is quoted in the same breath as blood avengers among American Indians, Maori, and Africans who have to taste the blood of their victims in order to lay their ghosts.[1] That is what our informants tell us; but to see no more in these customs than diverse expressions of a fear of ghosts which acts as a curb on would-be murderers is, from today's standpoint, almost ludicrous. What is significant for us in the Orestes story is that he murdered a *kinswoman*, that this kinswoman was his *mother*, and that his expiation was to mutilate himself by *biting off a finger*. To go to such an extreme merely to taste his own blood would have been silly. The parallels that leap to mind, for an anthropologist today, are other apparently irrational mutilations of the body carried out in the context of an overt or suppressed conflict between successive generations. We think of the strange story of Moses' wife Zipporah circumcising her son with a flint to save him from being killed by Yahweh,[2] and more particularly of the very

[1] J. G. Frazer, *Psyche's Task* (1913), p. 56.
[2] Exod. iv. 25.

9

widespread association of circumcision and other forms of mutilation with the initiation of youths and maidens into adulthood.

In short, we should now use the Orestes story not as one of a miscellany of examples to illustrate a particular kind of barbarous superstition, but as a model, or paradigm, from which we might be able to derive principles applicable in other cases.

In the same way Oedipus and Job both turn up in Frazer's *Folklore in the Old Testament*, but simply to illustrate widespread 'superstitious' customs. Job is cited, curiously enough, in evidence for the statement that in the Old Testament it is the blood of a murdered man, not his ghost, which cries out for vengeance, the reference being to Job's 'appealing against the injustice of his fate..."O earth, cover not my blood, and let my cry have no resting place"'.[1] As for Oedipus, he appears as a parallel to the story of Moses in the ark of bullrushes. He is one of many examples of the hero who was 'exposed at birth, and was only rescued from imminent death by what might seem to vulgar eyes an accident, but what really proved to be the finger of Fate interposed to preserve the helpless babe for the high destiny that awaited him...'.[2]

Fate, or Destiny, is the main theme of this essay.

[1] Frazer, *Folklore in the Old Testament* (1918 ed.), vol. I, p. 101.
[2] *Ibid.* vol. II, pp. 438–46.

It is mentioned in many places in Frazer's writings, and invariably in the manner I have described. There is no attempt to analyse the notion of Fate as a category of religious or philosophic thought. It is treated like any other customary belief—a belief in ghosts or in lucky and unlucky omens or in magical charms to fend off supernatural threats.

Supposing, however, that we consider the stories of Oedipus and Job from an analytical rather than a descriptive point of view.[1] What is notable then is that they epitomize, poignantly and dramatically, two religious and ethical conceptions that seem to be mutually opposed in some respects but complementary in others. These ideas are associated with different cosmological doctrines about the universe, and different conceptions of the nature of man and his relations with supernatural powers. I think that they represent, in a clear paradigmatic form, two fundamental principles of religious thought and custom. The Oedipal principle is best summed up in the notion of Fate or Destiny, the Jobian principle in that of Supernatural Justice.

Now I am not suggesting that the whole religious system of Greece of the fifth century B.C. can be reduced to what is represented in the story of Oedipus, or that the drama of Job contains the whole of Old Testament Hebrew religion. I am

[1] Cf. Meyer Fortes, 'Analysis and Description in Social Anthropology', *Advancement of Science* (1953), vol. XXXVIII.

concerned only with the specific conceptions em-
bodied in the two stories. That they are religious
conceptions is taken for granted by all our authorities,[1] and what I want to show is that they also
exist in West African religious systems.

[1] Cf. F. M. Cornford, *From Religion to Philosophy* (1912),
pp. 12 ff.; D. W. Lucas, *The Greek Tragic Poets* (1950),
pp. 133 ff.; J. Pedersen, *Israel: Its Life and Culture* (1926)
2 vols., pp. 358 ff.

CHAPTER II

OEDIPUS AND JOB AS PARADIGMS

THE myth of Oedipus is best known to us from the Theban plays of Sophocles; and what gives these plays their tragic intensity is not the horror they arouse of patricide and incest but the 'sense of the blindness and helplessness of mankind'[1] which, as Mr Lucas notes, they convey. The catastrophe which overwhelms Oedipus is due, Mr Lucas adds, to causes that 'lie hid deep in the nature of god and man', not to any faults of his.' On the contrary, he is a man of virtuous and noble character choosing self-imposed exile rather than risk slaying his supposed father, a just and benevolent king, a faithful husband and devoted father. And he has one further quality which in the end proves his downfall: his resolute pursuit of the truth. When he discovers the truth about his birth and marriage, he can only bear to live by blinding himself and so blotting out the intolerable knowledge. For his sins are so infamous that not even death could atone for them.

But it is not just a matter of his having committed them unwittingly. It is as if his actions have been

[1] Lucas, *op. cit.* pp. 133 ff.

thrust upon him, or he driven into them, by some agency operating outside the bounds of human knowledge and unresponsive to human conduct. He is the victim of Destiny. The question of responsibility or guilt does not even seem relevant. Much later, when as an old man he is preparing for death, in the *Oedipus Coloneus*, the question does come up and he asserts his innocence. It was an appalling Fate and not his own choosing.

The part played by the concept of Fate, which is the usual translation of the Greek word *Moira*, in early Greek religion has been much discussed by classical scholars.[1] It was clearly a very complex notion, but our authorities seem to be agreed that its original meaning was 'portion' or 'lot'. Furthermore, it seems to have had two aspects. One was the idea of Fate as an impersonal power representing the necessity and justice of the 'disposition of Nature', as Professor Dodds puts it, and supreme over both gods and men. The other was its reference to the individual. Each person is conceived of as having a particular apportionment of good and evil for his lifetime which is decided at birth; and 'this luck', to quote Professor Dodds again, 'is not conceived as an extraneous accident—it is as much part of a man's natal endowment as beauty or talent'.[2]

[1] E.g. Cornford, *op. cit.*; E. R. Dodds, *The Greeks and the Irrational* (1951); H. J. Rose, article, 'Fate', *Encyc. Brit.* 14th ed. [2] Dodds, *op. cit.* p. 42.

This is the aspect most conspicuous in the Oedipus myth. But we see there also that an individual's fate is in part determined by the fate of his parents and in turn affects that of his offspring. Professor Dodds relates this to the idea, very familiar to anthropologists from its occurrence in most primitive societies, that a son's life is the 'prolongation of his father's life'. By the laws of filiation and descent, a son who inherits his father's position in society *ipso facto* inherits both his material property and debts and his moral and ritual property and debts. Normally, however, filial succession is a deliberate and willing act. When Fate steps in, as with Oedipus, it occurs by blind and to some extent vainly resisted compulsion.

There is a similarity here to the notion of witch-craft.[1] Fate, like witchcraft, is an involuntary force and can, in the last resort, only be known in retrospect. This in itself generates efforts to discover it in advance and so to try to control it. Hence the appeal to oracles. But the oracles do not in fact enable men to master their fate. As with witch-craft, they merely help to reconcile men to its ineluctability. It is best of all, really, to accept this and not to seek arrogantly to probe destiny.

Job confronts us with a wholly different conception of man and of morality. There is no suggestion

[1] Cf. E. E. Evans-Pritchard, *Witchcraft, Oracles and Magic among the Azande* (1937).

here of inscrutable influences ruling the course of an individual's life from the moment of his birth. The good and evil that accrue to a man during his lifetime are the rewards and punishments meted out by an omnipotent, personified God. But God does not act arbitrarily or capriciously. He is, as Pedersen points out,[1] bound by a covenant with his creature, man. It is almost a contractual relationship, in which God is bound to act justly and mercifully, and man is free to choose between righteousness and sin. There is a known code of righteous conduct, and a man who has consistently followed the way of righteousness is entitled to well-being, peace of mind, happiness, and even material prosperity as a gift from the Supreme Ruler of the universe. Hence Job rejects the arguments and consolations of his friends. He will not admit that his afflictions are due to his having sinned, however inadvertently. He even feels entitled to demand of God 'shew me wherefore thou contendest with me',[2] and spurns the advice of his comforters to admit his guilt and recover his happiness by asking God's pardon.

It should be emphasized that all the characters in the story believe that God is just, that the righteous man must therefore prosper, and that 'the triumphing of the wicked is short'.[3] The question is whether Job's confidence in his own righteousness is justified

[1] Pedersen, *op. cit.* pp. 358 ff.
[2] Job x. 2.   [3] Job xx. 5.

or whether his calamities are evidence of unadmitted sin. And there is a still deeper question. Even if Job is justified in denying that he is wicked, does righteousness, as understood in terms of human conduct, create claims on God? Is not God all-powerful so that he stands above all human norms of good and bad conduct and is not bound by a concept of justice founded on a rule of reciprocal obligation? For God is not only the creator of the universe but the very source of righteousness and justice. And this is the gist of God's speech in the magnificent thirty-eighth to fortieth chapters. Man is not God's equal, and however virtuous he may feel himself to be, he cannot measure himself against God to disannul God's judgement and condemn Him in order to justify himself.[1]

It is when he realizes the import of this speech that Job is saved. He does not admit guilt in the sense of responsibility for actions that are wicked by ordinary human standards. What he admits is having placed himself on a footing of equality with God, judging for himself what conduct is righteous and what wicked. This wrong relationship was his sin. He accepts, as he has not previously done, the omnipotence of God and his own dependence on Him. Job's God is a majestic and all-powerful father-figure, the source of his creatures' life, and in virtue of that vested with final authority over them; and

[1] Job xl. 8.

reciprocally—as Job constantly pleads—with responsibility for their well-being and happiness. What Job has to learn is that God's authority is ultimate, inexplicable, not subject to coercion by obedience to rules of righteousness nor bound by contracts. Job's sufferings are like severe measures of discipline that a father might use to correct a son who, while exemplary in his conduct, was getting too big for his boots and arrogating to himself a status equal to his father's; and Job's salvation might be compared to the son's realizing and accepting his filial dependence. This means accepting paternal authority without resentment and seeing it as always benevolent in intention, even when it is used punitively. This is the essence of filial piety, and Job had been on the brink of acting in defiance of it.

CHAPTER III

THE NOTION OF FATE IN WEST AFRICA

THE notion of Fate or Destiny as an innate, though not necessarily impersonal determinant of an individual's life-history, and its complementary, the notion of Justice as the actions of a personified and deified agency responding to the individual's moral conduct and to his moral relationships with supernatural powers, can and do occur in a single religious system. Both seem to be present in some form in the theistic Western and Oriental religions.[1] It is the more interesting and instructive to find that both occur in the non-scriptural religious systems of many West African peoples. Indeed one of the characteristic marks of West African religions, as compared with other African religions (e.g. East and South African Bantu religions) in which ancestor-worship also plays a part, is the occurrence of the notion of Fate in them. What I wish to explore, with our paradigms to guide the inquiry, is how the two ideas are related in a West African religious system known to me at first hand.

[1] Cf. articles under 'Fate', in vol. v of Hastings's *Encyclopaedia of Religion and Ethics*.

But first let us take a few descriptive examples from other parts of West Africa. The Yoruba of Nigeria, Dr Bascom tells us,[1] associate a person's 'luck' with his 'destiny'. Luck is connected with the head and derives from one's 'creator' or spirit guardian. One man may work hard yet remain poor. This is because his luck is bad. Another man may work little yet get rich because his luck is good. Bad luck affects not only its owner but also those with whom he associates. As to Destiny, it is best to quote Dr Bascom's own words:

A person's luck and his success in economic and other affairs is also a matter of destiny (*ayanmope*, *ayanmo*) or fate (*iwa*) which is also known as 'to kneel and choose' (*akunleyan*). Before a child is born its soul is said to kneel before the deity (*Olodumare*) and choose (*yan*) its fate on earth. Those who humbly make reasonable requests for food, money or children receive what they ask during their life on earth. However those who make their requests as if they had the right to expect whatever they wanted, do not receive them....A person whose destiny on earth is poverty may be able to acquire some money by working hard, but he will never have very much. Diviners of various kinds...are consulted to find out what is in store for the future and what can be done to avert evil or insure a favourable outcome... but while the diviners may be able to recommend sacrifices (*ebo*) which will influence events in the immediate

[1] W. R. Bascom, 'Social Status, Wealth and Individual Differences among the Yoruba', *American Anthropologist* (1951), vol. LIII, no. 4.

future, they cannot alter the course of one's life or change his destiny.

Similar beliefs are held by the closely related people of Benin.[1] We learn that before he is born a person tells the Creator what he plans to do with his life and asks for the means to accomplish this. If he is unsuccessful he is said to be 'fighting against the fate which he has determined for himself'. Luck is associated with the head, so that a person is said to have 'a good head' or a 'bad head' according as he has been fortunate or not in his life, and he makes offerings to his head when he has a piece of good fortune.

These notions also form the core of the rich and complex cosmology and religious system of the Dahomeans, portrayed by Professor Herskovits.[2] Dahomean religion comprises three major categories of beliefs, mythology and associated cults: the worship of the ancestors, the worship of the great public deities, and the cult of personal gods and forces. These three categories are linked together by a 'complex and highly specialized system of divination' which is constantly resorted to for fatidical guidance and ritual advice. This system of divination is under the aegis of the cult of Fa, 'the destiny of the Universe as willed by the gods', as Professor

[1] Cf. R. E. Bradbury, *The Benin Kingdom* (Ethnographic Survey of Africa, part XIII, 1957).

[2] M. J. Herskovits, *Dahomey* (1938), vol. II, especially ch. xxx. See also B. Maupoil, *La Géomancie à l'ancienne Côte des Esclaves* (1943).

Herskovits interprets it. But Fa is also a personal Destiny whose worship, as might be expected in a society with so highly developed a patrilineal descent organization, is restricted to men. What is significant is that a man does not acquire his full Destiny until he is mature. As a boy, his father, after consulting a diviner, endows him with his partial Destiny symbolized in some palm-kernels which form the nucleus of a small shrine, and in specific food, clothing and other avoidances ascertained by the diviner. The incentive for a man to acquire his full Destiny is a series of misfortunes such as illness, the death of children or the barrenness of a wife. Women have only a partial Fa, as they are deemed to share the destiny of their fathers or husbands, since they are dependent on them in the same way as children are.

'What is in store for a man', says Professor Herskovits,[1] 'is foreordained.' Yet there is a way out through the 'divine trickster', Legba, the 'personification of Accident'. Legba is the messenger and spokesman of the gods and if he is properly propitiated he can divert predestined misfortunes. 'In this world ruled by Destiny', Professor Herskovits explains, 'man lives secure in the conviction that between the inexorable fate laid down for an individual and the execution of that fate lies the possibility of the way out....' There is also a 'way out'

[1] Herskovits, *op. cit.* vol. II, p. 222.

through the doctrine of the four souls. A man who reaches maturity achieves fulfilment of his life through his wives and children, his slaves and his entire household. His Destiny includes theirs, and this collective Destiny is watched over by his fourth soul. This is conceived as a kind of heavenly counterpart guarding an array of containers in which are stored good things like riches, health and children, and bad things like poverty, illness and death. The setting up of a man's full Destiny as a cult object is a ceremony for persuading this soul to select the good things of life for the individual.

To cap it all there is also the notion of Da, or luck, symbolized for the individual in the umbilicus and in cosmological terms by the snake and the rainbow. Da lies behind the vagaries of chance seen in particular incidents of good and ill luck. He pursues only men who have power and authority, such as heads of households or villages or kingdoms; and he manifests himself to them in the form of unexpected misfortunes which happen just when things are going particularly well. Hence he is regarded with apprehension. If he is neglected he becomes resentful and dangerous. A man learns through dreams or through a diviner that his Da desires to be established. If he is wise he establishes the Da in his house and worships it. This strengthens his luck and protects him against attacks from the Da of other men.

Brief as is this summary of Dahomean beliefs

concerning Fate and Destiny, it can be seen that they bear comparison with those of the Greeks. The Dahomeans also have an elaborate Pantheon of sky and earth gods headed by a creator divinity which is both male and female, and a complex ancestral cult correlated with descent groups, local communities and political units. The ancestors of a descent group are collectively enshrined and worshipped in a room specially set aside for this purpose. They are, as Professor Herskovits notes,[1] the focal point of the descent-group organization. Appeal is made to them through sacrifice and prayer to watch over the health and safety of any member of the group who is in hazard, and great ceremonial celebrations are held at set times, such as the harvest, to honour them. In very broad terms, therefore, their supernatural powers are called upon to safeguard the numbers and well-being of the descent group, whereas Destiny is involved in the play of chance in the individual's life-history.

The Yoruba, Bini and Dahomeans are closely related in culture. All have a complex system of ancestor-worship and a cult of gods or deified beings, together with the notion of Destiny. I have dwelt on their beliefs because they are characteristic of West Africa and the ethnographic data are so good. Similar patterns of cult and belief occur among other West African peoples, including some with no

[1] Herskovits, *op. cit.* vol. I, ch. XI.

obvious linguistic or cultural links with the Yoruba. The Tallensi, whose social and religious institutions I have studied in the field, are typical of one such non-Yoruba cluster.[1] I turn to them with a particular aim in mind. Generalized ethnographic descriptions have one serious defect. They do not enable us to see how ritual or belief is actually used by men and women to regulate their lives. A Tale friend once remarked to me, as he was going home from the funeral of a clan brother, 'Now that we have done the proper ritual our grief is soothed'. Another pointed out to me that when you consult a diviner you have the immediate relief of knowing what supernatural agency is causing your troubles and what ritual steps to take. It is only by considering it, in Malinowski's words,[2] as 'a mode of action as well as a system of belief, a sociological phenomenon as well as a personal experience' that the living meaning of ritual and belief becomes apparent. For this we must see religious ideas and rites in the context of the situation, the context of personal history and the context of social relationships: and these contexts can only be adequately supplied from one's own field observations.

[1] The Mole-Dagbane peoples of the Voltaic region. Cf. Meyer Fortes, *The Dynamics of Clanship among the Tallensi* (1945); *The Web of Kinship among the Tallensi* (1949).
[2] B. Malinowski, 'Magic, Science and Religion', in *Science, Religion and Reality*, ed. J. Needham (1925).

CHAPTER IV

THE TALLENSI: KINSHIP AND ANCESTOR CULT

THE religious institutions of the Tallensi cannot be understood without reference to their social organization. I have described this in detail else-where[1] and the barest summary must suffice here. We can begin with the domestic family living in its own homestead. This consists of a group of males, ideally a man and his adult sons and their sons, the wives of the adult men, and their unmarried daughters, in short a typical patrilineal joint family. The men of this family form a minor branch of a more extensive patrilineal lineage with common ancestry going back in some cases to ten or twelve generations. As the lineage is exogamous, the daughters marry out and the wives of its male members come from adjacent lineages. The lineage is a localized group with some political autonomy. But, as with the Dahomean descent group, its essential focus of unity and identity is the cult of the lineage ancestors. Just as there is a hierarchy of lineage segments of greater and greater inclusiveness, until finally the entire lineage is included, so there is a hierarchy of

[1] Fortes, *op. cit.* (1945, 1949).

ancestors and ancestor shrines. Members of the smallest segment worship the founding ancestors of their segment, join with the members of the next more inclusive segment to worship their common founding ancestors, and so on till the most inclusive unit, the maximal lineage as a whole, is reached. The lineage ancestor cult is by definition a cult of the patrilineal male ancestors. But the ancestress of a lineage or segment is almost as important as the founding ancestor, and the spirits of maternal ancestors and ancestresses play as big a part in a person's life as his paternal ancestor spirits.

In this social system, jural and ritual authority is vested in the men who have the status of fathers. Until a man's father dies he himself has no jural independence and cannot directly bring a sacrifice to a lineage ancestor. He is, as it were, merged in his father's status. Now paternal authority, however conscientiously and benevolently exercised, as it usually is among the Tallensi, inevitably gives rise to suppressed hostility and opposition in sons. This is quite explicitly recognized, and is dealt with by means of a number of ritual avoidances between a man and his first-born son. Indeed, so deep is the feeling of latent opposition between successive generations that ritual avoidances also hold between a woman and her first-born daughter.

Tale fathers are normally kind-hearted and tolerant, especially towards their young children, who are still in a stage of complete dependence on their parents. But when sons grow up and begin to farm for themselves and to look for wives, the wish for independence arises. Then the rights of the father—to command his son's labour and property, to take responsibility for him in law, to sacrifice on his behalf to ancestor spirits, to discipline his manners and morals—become irksome. The image emerges of the father as a taskmaster and minor despot. Tallensi say that a father's powers are absolute simply because he is his children's begetter. Whether he exercises his authority arbitrarily or benignly depends upon his own sense of duty, for there are no means open to children to constrain a father. A father who wishes to be respected, both by his own family and his kinsfolk and neighbours, should always make a just return to his son for his services and obedience.

A mother's rights are as absolute as a father's, but as women have no jural or economic or ritual authority, they take the form of moral claims upon, rather than jural power over, her children. A mother is thought of as a loving food-giver, ready to sacrifice herself for her children, their shield and comforter. This does not mean that mothers never discipline their children. On the contrary, it is they, not the fathers, who give children their earliest training in cleanliness, good manners and elementary morality. But they use persuasion where fathers give commands, they are content to scold where fathers are sometimes provoked to punish.

Thus the patterns of customary sentiment towards the father and the mother differ. But one inescapable duty rests on children in relation to both parents. This is the duty of filial piety. It requires a child to honour and respect his parents, to put their wishes before his own, to support and cherish them in old age, quite irrespective of their treatment of him. The supreme act of filial piety owed by sons is the performance of the mortuary and funeral ceremonies for the parents. It is felt by the Tallensi as a compulsion of conscience, but there is a powerful religious sanction in the background. To fail in it is to incur the everlasting wrath of the ancestors. For the mortuary and funeral rites are the first steps in the transformation of parents into ancestor spirits, and the worship of the ancestors is in essence the ritualization of filial piety.

Tale social life is almost wholly organized by reference to relations of descent and of kinship. Precise genealogical knowledge is necessary in order to define a person's place in society and his rights, duties, capacities and privileges. This is one reason why the cult of the ancestors is so elaborate amongst them. However, it is much more than a mnemonic for regulating their social relations. It is the religious counterpart of their social order, hallowing it, investing it with a value that transcends mundane

29

interests and providing for them the categories of thought and belief by means of which they direct and interpret their lives and actions. This is quite explicit. Every important activity and every significant social relationship among them is expressed and sanctioned by the ancestor cult. And the pivot of this cult is the key relationship in Tale social structure—that is, the relationship of father and son. Only men may offer sacrifice to the ancestors and a man cannot get ritual access to his forebears except through his father and mother. In his father's lifetime a man has no independent economic rights (for example, to land), or jural status (for example, in the matter of his marriage), except through his father; and it follows from this that he cannot officiate on his own account in religious rites. When his father dies and he succeeds to his father's place in society as an economically and jurally independent person he also becomes ritually adult. He is now able to sacrifice and pray to his patrilineal ancestors through his father who is amongst them. As maternal ancestors play an equally important part in Tale religion, the same rules apply with regard to the mother. In the most general terms, therefore, the ancestor cult is the transposition to the religious plane of the relationships of parents and children; and that is what I mean by describing it as the ritualization of filial piety.

Filial piety is in fact a kind of regulating mechanism in the relations of parents and children. Custom defines sons as their fathers' eventual supplanters but puts them in their fathers' absolute power. The hostility that this might generate is drained away in the ritual avoidances binding on an eldest son (who represents all his brothers). He may not eat with his father or wear his clothes or use his bow or enter his granary. He breaks these taboos in a solemn ritual during the final funeral ceremonies for his father. A father should exercise his authority benevolently. If he does not his sons may be tempted to revolt and leave him. But filial piety binds them to accept paternal authority no matter how it is exercised, and they very rarely do revolt. If they do, usually on the grounds of economic necessity, they normally return to their father's home after his death, in submission to the mystical powers which he now has as an ancestral spirit.

Descent and kinship fix a person's place in society, and the rights, duties and capacities consequential to it, in terms of his membership of such groups as the lineage and the family, and of his relations with other kin through his parents, spouses, children. But there is another pole of existence for him. There is the fact of his individuality. To be sure, in this homogeneous society every life-history is much the same, allowing for differences of sex and age. Yet every life-history is also unique. Some men achieve the supreme ends of life—health, longevity and above all children to perpetuate their line of descent and care for them after death. Others do not. Each life is a particular fabric of good and ill, even though it is woven of fibres common to all. Meaning is given to this fact too in the ancestor cult.

The beliefs and practices of Tale ancestor-worship fit precisely into their social structure. We should note, first, that Tallensi are confronted with their ancestors in a very material way, for every homestead is full of shrines dedicated to the ancestor spirits. These shrines, built of dried mud and covered with a variety of relics and other ritual paraphernalia, differ markedly in appearance, for each type symbolizes a specific category, or configuration, of ancestor spirits. Tallensi explain that these shrines and objects are not inhabited by their ancestors, but represent them and form the altars where men can get into contact with them. In their prayers Tallensi always call on a particular group of ancestors, each by his or her name, to attend at their shrine to accept sacrifices.

Tallensi make contact with their ancestors by means of sacrifices, libations and prayers, but they only take such ritual action after consulting a diviner. The diviner reveals which configuration of ancestors is involved in the situation at issue, and what sacrifices are demanded by them. Diviners are consulted by and on behalf of both individuals and groups at family crises like child-birth, sickness or death, at public crises like drought, at seasonal and ceremonial turning points like sowing and harvest times, before hazardous undertakings like setting off for a hunt, and whenever the mood takes a responsible man. Thus the ancestor spirits are continuously involved in the affairs of the living; but they manifest their powers and interest characteristically in the unforeseeable occurrences which upset normal expectations and routines; and they do so in order to make some demand or elicit submission. These occurrences are sometimes deemed fortunate by their descendants, though more often they are experienced as unfortunate. Furthermore, ancestors manifest themselves in different ways for men and for women and with different effect at the successive stages of the individual's life.

CHAPTER V

LIFE-CYCLE AND OEDIPAL DESTINY

IF we consider any person's life-history, the essential starting point is the mere fact that he was born alive and survived to live. The Tallensi conceptualize this in their ancestor cult by the notion of the spirit guardian (*sɛɣr*). Soon after a child's birth its father ascertains through a diviner which of his ancestors, associated with which configuration of ancestral powers, desires to take this child as its ward; and what the spirit guardian does is simply to watch over and try to preserve his ward's life itself.

The case of Dentiya illustrates this. One day he brought a sheep to be sacrificed to his spirit guardian. It appeared that in the past few years his first wife had died, his second wife had lost her baby and now his third wife was pregnant. A diviner had revealed that all this was the doing of his spirit guardian. The spirit guardian declared that he had preserved Dentiya's life through many trials, but that Dentiya had neglected him. Therefore he had caused the death of his wife and child. Now that the third wife was pregnant, the spirit guardian demanded, first, reparation, and then the custody of the unborn child. The sheep was an offering of reparation, acquiescence, and conciliation given with prayers for the safe birth of the unborn babe, the welfare of its mother, and the health and prosperity of its father and his kin. In this case Dentiya was the ward of his patrilineal lineage ancestors grouped together in the configuration of the supreme lineage *bɔyar*,[1] and the offering was made by the head of his lineage segment on the shrine dedicated to them. But all categories of ancestors take children as their wards. Furthermore, offerings are always made to a person's spirit guardian at decisive stages of the life-cycle. A man takes a fowl or a guinea-fowl to be offered to his wife's spirit guardian by her father when she is advanced in pregnancy; and, most important of all, a person's spirit guardian must be informed as soon as he dies, for the life watched over is now ended.

But life—symbolized for the Tallensi in the breath (*ɲovor*)—is only the raw material for living. What one makes of it depends on other spiritual agencies. Let us take an extreme but common enough type of case. The six-year-old child of a close friend of mine suffered from a long, wasting illness. Medicines had been tried in vain and diviners had attributed the sickness to the anger of various ancestors who had been approached with promises

[1] Cf. Fortes, *Dynamics of Clanship*, pp. 52 ff.

of the prescribed offerings if the child should recover. But the child died. At the divination which always forms part of the mortuary ceremony, it emerged that the cause of death was the child's mother's Prenatal Destiny (*Nuor-Yin*). A six-year-old's social identity is so merged in that of its parents, more particularly its mother's, that what happens to it is interpreted as deriving from *her* relationship with spiritual agencies. At about the same time a youth of about eighteen died of a similar wasting illness and it was revealed that it was due to his own *Nuor-Yin*, he being mature enough to have an individual social identity. But when his twenty-five-year old, newly married half-brother died of acute dysentery, divination ascribed it to the configuration of the lineage ancestors assembled at the supreme lineage shrine. And these differences in the attribution of the mystical causation of death, so obviously corresponding to the position of the individual in the social structure, are also reflected in the grief of the bereaved and in the range of kinsfolk and clansfolk concerned. When a small infant dies, the funeral rites are quickly over and only the closest kinsfolk and clansfolk of the parents attend; but when a lineage elder dies the funeral rites are elaborate and protracted and all the clans of the neighbourhood, as well as a very wide range of kinsfolk and affines, take part.

However, the full significance of Prenatal Destiny

is clearest from the way it affects women. In Tale eyes no one is so unfortunate or so unhappy as a woman who has no children. If, as happens only too often, a young wife loses her babies one after another by miscarriage or in early infancy, she becomes chronically miserable and dejected, and her husband too, for that matter. It is then suspected, and diviners soon confirm, that the cause is her evil Prenatal Destiny. But while there's life there's hope, and, as elsewhere in West Africa, there is a customary way out of the dilemma. There is a ritual procedure for exorcizing Prenatal Destiny in cases of this sort. The rites are carried out by the woman's *father's* lineage, but at her married home, and the logic underlying the procedure is clearly expressed in the prayers. First a sacrifice is offered to her lineage ancestors. They are adjured to drive out the evil Prenatal Destiny. For was it not through their beneficence that she was born their child and was, moreover, born a woman? They must see to it that her womanhood is fulfilled. She was properly married, bride-price had been received for her and her husband had a right to have children by her. What else is marriage for? A woman's offspring have close relationships of affection, duty and privilege with her paternal kin and receive essential ritual services from them. Her paternal ancestors receive cattle of her bride-price in sacrifice. More than that, they receive ritual service from her offspring. Thus

37

they benefit from her fertility both materially and
spiritually, in ways that are directly parallel to and
conditional upon the benefits her husband's kin
receive from it. In justice to all, therefore, she must
be enabled to bear children. After this follows a
magical ceremony in which the woman is purged by
washing, and the Prenatal Destiny is symbolically
drawn off and cast away.

It is easy to see that a woman's Prenatal Destiny
is linked with her filial status in her own lineage.
For it is through being born a girl in her own lineage
that she is endowed with fertility and it is through
having been brought up to maturity by her parents
that she is able to put her child-bearing powers at
the disposal of her husband's lineage. When, more
rarely, a man is the victim of Prenatal Destiny the
symptom is usually failure, through some infirmity,
to marry or to make a livelihood. Then his own
lineage, assisted by members of his mother's lineage,
perform the exorcism. He is their offspring and his
native endowment derives from his birth and upbringing. If it has failed him, only his or their
ancestors have the mystical power to save him.

What then is this Prenatal Destiny? Tallensi have
a clear doctrine. The ultimate source of everything
on earth is Heaven (*Naawun*). But there are no
myths giving an account of the creation, or as they
say, pouring out (*bah*) of the world, and no shrines
for worship of Heaven. He or It is simply the Final

Cause of everything that exists. Before it is born a child is 'with Heaven', not in any literal sense but in the symbolical sense of being in process of creation. At that time it declares its wishes to Heaven—hence the term *Nuor-Yin*, literally Spoken Destiny. It may declare that it does not wish to have parents or a spouse or children or farms or livestock. This means that it rejects ordinary human living though it cannot avoid being born. This is its evil Prenatal Destiny; and sometimes this is so powerful that its owner dies or else causes illness and even death to a parent, spouse or child.

Very similar notions occur in other parts of West Africa, as we have already seen, but placing them in their context of situation and social organization throws significant light on them. For one thing, they explain and provide customary reassurance against the impact of diseases and failures that defy the knowledge and skill of the people. Thus it is very obvious to an observer that the ritual of exorcism brings relief and hope to the sufferers, as well as to their kin. But most serious disease is intractable by the magical and religious techniques which are the basis of all Tale cures. A further element comes in. The victims of Prenatal Destiny are a selected type. They are all out on a limb, or potentially so, in the social structure, being either too young to be implicated in responsible tasks and social relations or having apparently incurable physical or psychological defects that put them in danger of leaving no children and of thus eventually becoming socially forgotten. It seems that in these circumstances the notion of Prenatal Destiny serves as a legitimate alibi. It relieves the sufferer's kin, and therefore society at large, of responsibility and guilt for his troubles and, indeed, exonerates him in his own eyes. For he is not aware that he is the victim of his Prenatal Destiny until this is revealed by a diviner.

CHAPTER VI

GOOD DESTINY, ANCESTOR SPIRITS AND PARENTS

THE notion of Prenatal Destiny among the Tallensi is, clearly, a simpler version of Oedipal Fate. There is, however, also another aspect of Destiny. In this, benevolence predominates; it does not commonly become effective till adolescence; and it pertains to men only. So every married man has his Good Destiny (*Yin*) shrine. While he is still young and dependent on his father, it stands in his mother's quarters. Later when he has children it is moved to his wife's quarters. And finally, when he succeeds to his father's place, it is moved outside to show that it owns and guards the whole family group. It is, in fact, a ritual record of a man's life-history. It begins with his emergence from infancy on to the threshold of adult jural status, and grows step by step as his involvement in responsible social relations expands through marriage, fatherhood, economic independence, family headship and lineage eldership. Women are not independently endowed with Destiny in this sense because they have no jural or religious autonomy. As daughters and sisters in their parental family and lineage they are under the authority, and are the responsibility, of their fathers. As wives and mothers in their conjugal families they come under their husband's power. A woman's life-cycle is therefore interpreted as being governed first by her father's and subsequently by her husband's Destiny.

A man's Good Destiny springs ultimately from his unknown prenatal wishes and is sometimes spoken of as if it were the universal Heaven entering into the life and achievements of the individual. But it manifests itself through what we should call accidents and coincidences. This follows a completely stereotyped pattern; only the combination of elements in the pattern is unique for each individual. As Tallensi say, everybody gets ill sometimes, marries, has children, kills animals in the hunt, and so forth. Why then should illness strike a particular person at a particular time? Why should one man be fortunate in his marriages and have many children while his brother fails in these respects? One cannot foresee the course of one's life, for it is governed by forces beyond human knowledge and control; and these Tallensi conceptualize in terms of their ancestor cult. Thus each person's total life-history is unique, though the events it is made up of are similar to those of other people's lives; and its particular course depends on his Destiny. That is why an offering to a *Yin* shrine is often eaten only by the owner and his wife and children, his kin by birth not being allowed to share in it as in his other sacrifices.

Let us consider a few examples. As a youth of sixteen or so, Zaŋ went out herding his father's cattle one day. Coming to a pool, he saw a crocodile on the bank and promptly shot it. It was taken home and eaten by the elders. Zaŋ's father, as was his duty, went to consult a diviner about the incident. He revealed that it was a manifestation of Zaŋ's Destiny. It was his father's father and *his* mother who were manifesting themselves in the crocodile and the arrow which had killed it. They were Zaŋ's Destiny. He must set up a shrine and sacrifice to them, and they would watch over his well-being. So a small shrine was built of clay, the skull of the crocodile and the arrow which slew it being embedded in it as symbols of the ancestors who had chosen Zaŋ. At first Zaŋ's father always made offerings on his behalf. After his father's death, Zaŋ did this for himself.

This is a typical history of the beginnings of a man's Destiny shrine. Another, illustrating a different aspect of the notion, is Kunyaaŋba's. When he first began to farm like a grown man, at the age of about sixteen, a sickness of the feet laid him low. His father went to a diviner and it appeared that it was due to *his* father and father's father manifesting themselves as the boy's Destiny. The sickness had been a sign that they demanded to be accepted as

his Destiny, his hoe being the material symbol of
their interest and will. Furthermore, it was their
wish that he should never eat any grain he himself.
cultivated. This is a very inconvenient personal
taboo in the household economy of the Tallensi and
Kunyaaŋba at first jibbed at it. He was cured and
went on farming. Then he became ill again, more
seriously. This time divination revealed that his
Destiny ancestors were angry at his defiance and
now required him never to use a hoe, that is, to give
up farming completely. This was a great blow, as
there are no alternative equally rewarding occupa-
tions for an energetic and capable young man. But
there was no choice, for to disobey would mean to
risk illness or even death for himself, his wife or his
children. This taboo was one of the reasons why
Kunyaaŋba went to work abroad. But he felt it as a
serious privation. He spoke of it reluctantly, as if he
felt ashamed, emphasizing that there was no redress.

Such personal taboos are often imposed by
Destiny ancestors. They may forbid their wards
from wearing cloth garments, from eating certain
foods, from cutting their hair, from doing certain
kinds of work, and so forth. These taboos are
scrupulously observed for the wages of disobedience
is misfortune, sickness and even the death of a wife
or child. It is significant that Destiny ancestors
rarely cause the death of their ward. This ultimate
sanction is generally used against his dependants (as

God did with Job) as a means of bringing the ward himself to heel. For Destiny is, ideally, beneficent, provided only that the ward accepts his Destiny ancestors, serves them and obeys them. He shows this by faithfully keeping the taboos they impose, however arbitrary and inconvenient they may be from the rational point of view of normal Tale life.

Yet another aspect of Destiny appears in the case of Luoni. He slew a fully grown male crocodile at a distant river. It proved to be the vehicle of his Destiny ancestors. Ever since, he is woken up from time to time by a nightmare in which he sees himself pursued by the crocodile. He gets up, seizes a rattle, and runs in the night to the path leading to the river, then on to his mother's brother's home whence his Destiny ancestors originate, and this dispels the attack. His family takes no notice, for, as his son said, 'It is his affair; we have nothing to do with it.' A man's Destiny often asserts itself in this way when it was originally acquired through the killing of a big game animal. And it persists until the final establishment of the shrine. This takes place in the later years of life when his household, his children and his survival are the tangible evidences of the beneficence of his Destiny. An elderly man frequently learns through diviners that his Destiny demands the sacrifice of a cow in gratitude for long continued favours, and when this sacrifice is offered it is a triumphant occasion.

A man's Destiny, then, consists of a unique configuration of ancestors who have of their own accord
elected to exercise specific surveillance over his life-
cycle, and to whom he is personally accountable. No
one else, not even his brother, has the same configuration of Destiny ancestors.[1] They are always immediate forbears and most commonly paternal in
character. They first manifest themselves through
a critical experience or achievement at an appropriate
stage of a man's life-cycle. It may be an illness;
often it is through a productive achievement like
slaying a game animal for the first time or excelling
in farming. The material relics of these events form
the shrine dedicated to the Destiny ancestors. In
return for his submission and service, a man's
Destiny is supposed to preserve his health, his life
and the well-being of his family, to bring him good
fortune in his economic activities and social aspira-
tions, and to confer on him, in due course, the
immortality of ancestorhood by blessing him with
sons and grandsons.

This is the supreme evidence of the goodwill of
his ancestors, and the special power of Destiny in
this matter is shown in two significant ways. First,
though all categories of ancestors can and, as I have
already mentioned, do elect to be the spirit guardians
of a man's children, his Destiny ancestors pre-
dominate among them. Thus the most enduring

[1] Cf. Fortes, *The Web of Kinship*, pp. 229 ff.

fulfilment of a man's role in the social structure is identified with his Good Destiny.

Secondly, there is the appeal to Destiny in interpreting the ambivalence in the relationship of fathers and sons. Fathers want and need sons to perpetuate their social existence. But they become increasingly loth to yield their place to their sons as their bodily and social capacities wane and those of their sons wax with the passage of time. Sons accept their dependent status with affectionate respect and filial piety; but with every step towards jural autonomy, especially after they marry and have children, they chafe increasingly at their father's authority. Beneath the solidarity due to common interests and mutual dependence lies the rivalry and opposition of successive generations. This is what generates the tensions symbolized and drained away in the taboos of the first-born. Tallensi explain it by means of the notion of Destiny. They say that a father's Destiny and his first-born son's Destiny are hostile to each other. During the son's infancy the father's Destiny is superior. As the son grows up, physically and socially, his Destiny grows stronger; indeed, it is because his Destiny is strong enough that the son succeeds in growing up. This is a threat to the father's Destiny. Father's Destiny and son's Destiny are enemies; each wishes to destroy the other so that its protégé may be master of the house and free to give it sacrifices and service. For this reason a married first-born son with children of his own is forbidden to use the same gateway as his father lest they meet face to face, Destiny against Destiny. This is reminiscent of the fatal effects an evil Pre-destiny may have on its victim's parents or children. The implication is that a person's Destiny (or, as the Greeks might have said, daemon), both in its malign form and in its benign form, asserts itself in opposition to that of his parents, or rather of his father, since his mother's is ruled by his father's.

Remembering that a son finally wins jural and ritual independence only on the death of his father, we must conclude that this is a victory for the son's Destiny. It is inevitable, yet Tallensi do not admit it. To do so would make the stabilizing effect of the first-born's taboos nugatory and destroy the very basis of the relationship between successive generations. Instead they emphasize the supreme filial duty of performing a parent's funeral rites. The effect of these is to transform the dead father (and, by the same principle, the mother) into an ancestor spirit and re-establish him in his family in his spiritual status. This transforms his mundane and material jural authority into mystical power—that is, power which is absolute, autocratic and unpredictable because it transcends the human controls of moral and jural sanctions. It is as if fathers are exorbitantly compensated by society with spiritual powers for being deprived of material powers for the sake of the continuity of the society. It reconciles them with their sons who have ousted them and exonerates the latter of guilt, as can be discerned in the symbolism of the funeral ceremonies and in Tale beliefs about the ultimate causes of death, to which I will presently come.

What, then, is the service due to one's Good-Destiny ancestors? In form it is just like the service due to any other ancestors in whatever configuration they are worshipped. First, they must be accepted[1] and enshrined. This takes place at their behest, conveyed through a diviner. It takes place according to the usual pattern, that is, as a result of misfortunes or coincidences which are interpreted as the manifestations of the ancestors. Being enshrined, the ancestors are restored in spirit form to the homes and hearths from which death cut them off in their physical form. They will continue to assert their power by causing troubles, but the means of placating them (and of thus allaying the anxieties and the disturbances of routine expectations due to their interventions) will be at hand. Secondly, they must receive regular offerings and libations. Tallensi interpret this as giving them food and drink, and

[1] There is a special term (*say*) in the ritual language of the Tallensi for accepting, or rather consenting to, the commands of ancestors, and it is noteworthy that the same word is used to describe the action of a parent, an elder or an ancestor when he is thought to be responding benevolently to the conduct of a dependant.

49

thus expressing filial reverence and commemoration. And it is significant that this service is also normally given only in response to demands consequent on a warning misfortune or threat of misfortune. This applies even to sacrifices at fixed seasonal and ceremonial times, like the harvest. Every household head then sacrifices to all his ancestor shrines, but only in accordance with the demands received through a diviner. Thirdly, there is the observance of taboos which symbolize submission to the ancestors and compliance with the norms and customs instituted by them. In this aspect the fearful quality of the ancestors, particularly Destiny and Divining-ancestors, becomes apparent. It is manifested directly in the case of Destiny ancestors in nightmares which can be allayed only by an act of quasi-ritual obedience, and indirectly in the anxious anticipation of supernatural afflictions for disobedience. Destiny ancestors are benevolent not out of affection for their descendants but out of self-interest and because they have the power. Their solicitude is gained not by demonstrations of love but by proofs of loyalty.

What distinguishes the worship of Destiny from that of other ancestor configurations is the fact already mentioned, that it is a unique ritual relationship not shared, as are other ritual relationships, with kinsfolk and clansfolk. Tallensi have a shrewd understanding of individual differences in character and disposition; but this does not lead them to perceive individuality as a growth from within. Both to himself and to others the individual is what he sees himself to have achieved; and every significant achievement is credited to the good-will of his Destiny. It supports him by bringing him luck, which the Tallensi, like the other West African peoples cited, associate with the head. It also aids him by warding off adversity. In Tale thought everything that happens has material causes and conditions, but they are effective only by grace of the mystical agencies which are the ultimate arbiters of nature and society. So they say that if a man wishes to prosper he must have skill, industry and thrift. But these are not enough; without the beneficence of Destiny they will be abortive; and even this is not enough, for behind Destiny is the collective power of all the ancestors, notably that of the omnipotent lineage ancestors.

In this special relationship of a man with his Destiny ancestors (as in his relationships with all his ancestors) morality in the sense of righteous conduct does not count. All that matters is service and obedience. A man who is wicked by Tale standards may flourish while his virtuous brother is a failure. But even assiduous service is not a guarantee of success. The ancestors are easily, and mostly inadvertently, offended, and this cannot be known until something goes wrong. That is why even fixed ceremonial occasions are potentially hazardous. It may then transpire that one group of ancestors has taken offence because they were overlooked in favour of some other group. Ancestors thus incensed may override a man's Destiny and bring disaster upon him. Divination after a death often reveals such a story. The result is that when a sacrifice is offered to any one configuration of ancestors, offerings must also be given, as advised by the diviner, to all the other ancestors in the officiant's custody. Thus if the main sacrifice is to be given to a man's Destiny shrine he will first make the rounds of the other ancestor shrines in his possession. These will include his father's Destiny, his own divining shrine, the shrine dedicated to his mother if she is dead, and, if he is of sufficient seniority, the shrine of the lineage ancestors. Each receives a small sacrifice, perhaps only a libation of water, is told the circumstances of the occasion and is besought to show good-will. Tallensi account for this by referring to kinship. As a jural minor in your father's lifetime you need the consent, or at least the blessing, of your father and often of your lineage elders in order to undertake anything important for yourself. You must also tell your mother out of respect for her. The same pattern holds for transactions with your ancestors.

It is worth noting that this plurality of ancestral powers, thought of as competing unpredictably in their demands on their worshippers, actually works as a safeguard in everyday affairs. Since there is no single, sovereign god like Job's, one cannot feel entitled to rewards for following a code of conduct pleasing to him or deserving of punishment for knowingly transgressing it. One lives according to one's mundane lights, guided by the jural and moral sanctions of society, knowing that the ancestors dispense justice by their own standards and that one cannot please all of them at the same time.

Here there is an apparent inconsistency in Tale thought. For the ancestors are not considered to be wholly indifferent to moral values. On the contrary, they are the jealous guardians of the highest moral values, that is to say, the axiomatic values from which all ideal conduct is deemed to flow. The first is the rule that kinship is binding in an absolute sense. From this follows the second rule, that kinship implies amity in an absolute sense. The third rule is the fundamental one. It postulates that the essential relationship of parent and child, expressed in the parent's devoted care and the child's affectionate dependence, may never be violated and is, in that sense, sacred. It is indeed the source of the other rules. Tallensi believe that anyone who violates these rules is liable to the ultimate mystical penalty of death. For though every death has material causes, no death can occur except by the will of the ancestors.

We can see what the issue is. It is not a question

53

of morality in the sense of righteous conduct. It is not a matter of, say, dealing honestly with one's neighbours, refraining from adultery, never committing a murder. Virtue in these matters does not earn the blessings of the ancestors and a wrongdoer will escape their wrath unless his actions are also transgressions of the rule of kinship amity. It is a question of moral relationships, not of good deeds. What the ancestors demand and enforce on pain of death is conformity with the basic moral axioms in fulfilling the requirements of all social relationships; and these are the counterpart, in the domain of kinship, of the obligations posited between persons and their ancestors in the religious domain. This is understandable since the latter are derived from the former by extension and transposition to the religious domain.

The point I am concerned with here is well illustrated by the story of Pu-ɛŋ-yii. Tempted by the opportunity of gain, he deserted his own patrilineal kin to ally himself with a rival lineage. Then, at the height of his prosperity, he was involved in a lorry accident. Luckily he escaped with a badly injured leg. On consulting a diviner he learnt that his mishap was brought about by his lineage ancestors. Deserting his paternal kin was a sin, for it meant that he could not join with them in true amity in sacrifices to his fathers and forefathers. This was tantamount to forsaking his ancestors and in their

anger they meant to kill him. However, said the
diviner, his Destiny was propitious and had inter-
ceded to save his life. He must apologize to his
lineage elders, offer up a sheep to his lineage ancestors to show his contrition and submission, and
make a sacrifice of thanksgiving to his Destiny. He
must also forthwith give up his association with the
rival lineage. Pu-ɛŋ-yii was a sophisticated, much-
travelled and commercially minded man; but he
immediately complied, believing that death would
be the penalty of refusing.

CHAPTER VII

THE SUPREMACY OF THE LINEAGE ANCESTORS

IN the religious system of the Tallensi the lineage ancestors have the last word. They are a person's or a group's fathers and forefathers by strict patrilineal descent from a founding ancestor and his wife to a deceased father. They are omnipotent, but not uniformly benevolent or malevolent. They are just;[1] and their justice is directed to enforcing the moral and religious norms and values on which the social order rests. They do this through the power over life and death in which they are supreme. Life, which surpasses all other forms of the good, and death which is the end of everything, as the Tallensi phrase it, are dispensed by the ancestors by what can best be described as the right of primordial parenthood. Their powers are those of a father immeasurably magnified and sanctified—that is, removed from the controls of co-operation and reciprocity, conscience and love as they work in the life

[1] This is the attribute that distinguishes ancestors from other supernatural agencies in most religious systems which include the worship of ancestors. Cf. Monica Wilson, *Rituals of Kinship among the Nyakusa* (1956), for a striking analysis of this conception among an East African people.

of the family. They have this character in the specific configuration of the lineage ancestors with their special shrines. It will be remembered that a lineage ancestor can also become manifest in other configurations.

How then does their justice work? Take the case of a daughter of a lineage who is persecuted by an evil Prenatal Destiny. Whether or not she can be rid of it depends upon the will of her lineage ancestors. It is in their interest that there shall be children and children's children to keep the social order in being and to serve and commemorate them. And this may weigh more in the balance of ancestral justice than sins of omission or commission. Or take the case of a man who is fortunate in his Good Destiny and has a long and successful life. In the end his day, too, comes, as the Tallensi say, and he must die. The material cause, there for all to see, may be old-age or disease; the exact moment and circumstances are the will of the ancestors. However virtuous, respected and devout he may have been, his death is invariably interpreted as the consequence of a failure in his or his predecessors' piety towards his ancestors. It may be due to some long-forgotten sin, his own or his father's, which he and his kin had thought of as having been expiated but which now, in retrospect, proves to be still resented by the ancestors. Or it may be an apparently commonplace ritual debt —and even the best of men have such debts at all

times. Sometimes they are known to a man's sons
and brothers, often they are not. For instance,
every man of seniority has ritual obligations arising
out of his status in his lineage and in society. Since,
however, Tallensi think of an offering as a response
to a demand from the ancestors, not as a spontaneous
gift, they are very apt to put off these obligations.
The demand may come with the usual sign of illness,
chance mishap or even a stroke of luck. But it may
not be revealed until death overtakes a man or one
of his dependants. Thus every mature man knows
that he must some day complete the enshrinement
of his Destiny ancestors. But he will procrastinate,
thinking that it will be time enough when he gets
older and there are children and grandchildren to
prove the benevolence of his Destiny. This is a
known obligation. If he dies before fulfilling it, it
may be the mystical cause of his death. Diviners
will disclose that his ingratitude had angered his
Destiny ancestors, who had slain him with the consent
of his lineage ancestors. Again, a man who succeeds
to the custody of a lineage shrine may in good faith
postpone the taking-over ceremony until he has
enough grain for beer and livestock for the sacrifices.
If he dies in the meanwhile this delay may be revealed as the mystical cause. Then there is the 'cow
of the bride-price' which a man owes to his lineage
ancestors when he has married off all his daughters,
and putting off this sacrifice may end in his death

or in that of one of his dependants. It may not even until he has long passed away.

In short, however conscientious a man may be in discharging his ritual obligations, there is always a loophole. For the will of the ancestors only becomes known after they strike, the range of ancestors who can manifest themselves in order to assert their rights is extraordinarily wide, and ritual debts to ancestors pass on from generation to generation. The system as a whole is impregnable, particularly since the criterion invoked is ritual service, not conduct that can be judged by men themselves. Whatever the ancestors do must therefore be, and is, accepted as just, and men have no choice but to submit. The parallel with Job is obvious. But unlike the Biblical hero, Tallensi do not attempt to dispute their ancestors' rights and authority, though they commonly plead with them for benevolence and sometimes protest their own deserts.

CHAPTER VIII

JUSTICE, RESPONSIBILITY AND THE ANCESTRAL CULT

TALE religious beliefs and practices, like those of other peoples, serve a cathartic purpose. The grief, anger and anxiety aroused by the afflictions of material loss or sickness or death are assuaged by them. But this is not the aspect of their religious system which concerns us here. What is of interest to us is the deeper catharsis, social as well as individual, made possible by the fusion in their religious system of Oedipal and Jobian notions.

I am thinking particularly of the question of fixing responsibility for the vicissitudes of life. Beliefs in witchcraft, magic and sorcery have a relatively minor place in Tale thought, in contrast to many other African religions.[1] Tale cosmology is wholly dominated by the ancestor cult. Even the elaborate totemic institutions, the cult of the Earth[2] and the beliefs about the dangerous mystical qualities of evil trees, animals and other natural phenomena

---

[1] Cf. Fortes, *Web of Kinship*, pp. 32 ff. In this respect the Tallensi are very different from the other West African societies I have referred to.

[2] Cf. Fortes, *Dynamics of Clanship*, ch. VIII.

are subordinated to it. The result is that it is inconceivable for Tallensi to attribute serious misfortune to the sole agency of a witch, a medicine or a mystically 'bad' tree or animal. The final arbitrament rests with the ancestors. This means that ultimate responsibility is projected outside the living body politic, not on to neighbours or kinsfolk or natural phenomena, as happens in societies with extensive witchcraft and magical beliefs.[1] But this does not wipe out human responsibility entirely. What ancestor-worship provides is an institutionalized scheme of beliefs and practices by means of which men can accept some kind of responsibility for what happens to them and yet feel free of blame for failure to control the vicissitudes of life. The moral responsibility for the manifestations of Destiny or the ancestors is always fixed on the person (or his jural superior) who is their object. When he accepts and later enshrines the ancestors who manifest themselves for him, or when he admits failure in service and makes reparation by sacrificing to them, he is accepting his own responsibility. But there is an implication of duress in this; and the very act of acquiescing in his own moral responsibility estab-

---

[1] As in the classical case of the Azande (cf. E. E. Evans-Pritchard, *op. cit.*). Cf. also Monica Wilson, *op. cit.* and an illuminating discussion of the same point by Professor P. Mayer in his paper *Witches*, Rhodes University, Grahamstown, 1957.

lishes the final, mystical responsibility of the ancestors.

The result is that the Tallensi can accept responsibility on the personal level for the good and ill in their lives without feeling morbidly guilty or having guilt fixed on them by jural and religious sanctions. Indeed, a striking feature of Tale response to misfortune is the absence of customary expressions of guilt, though grief, anger, anxiety, despair, and the comforting emotions of hope and relief, are freely demonstrated.

Putting it in another way, we could say that when things go wrong a person admits that he is in some sense answerable. But he is allowed, nay compelled, by custom to perceive his misfortunes as emanating in the last resort from his ancestors. Since they are invested with personality they can be appeased by word and act, and this serves to restore both the sufferer's self-trust and his social esteem.

The mechanism of this is clear. By enshrining his ancestors and so taking them back into his home and his life a man gains direct access to them. By accepting the duty of preserving and caring for them he converts their potential hostility to potential friendship. It is not a contractual relationship, as some authorities say is the case with Job, but one of mutual interdependence and obligation, albeit an uneasy one, fraught with the constant possibility of mischance due to the incommensurable capacities and powers of the parties. It is, in fact, a re-establishment on a new plane of the filio-parental interdependence severed by death. For death is the culmination of the cleavage between successive generations that is basic to Tale social structure. In ancestor-worship it is transcended, and conceptually as well as emotionally reversed. The parents, metamorphosed into ancestors, are restored to a place in their children's life that reflects, in symbolic form, critical attributes of parenthood in real life. Real parents demand obedience, economic services, respect which goes so far, in special cases, as to turn into obligatory avoidance, as well as affectionate trust. Ancestors demand ritual services, sacrifices, reverence, and taboo avoidances. Real parents have economic power and jural authority over their children and possess knowledge and skill which seem immeasurably great to their children while they are young. Perpetuated in supernatural form, these attributes become mystical power and authority, ubiquity and omnipotence. On the other hand, and this is equally important, real parents not only command and make demands on their children; they also care for them with affection and self-sacrifice. Ancestors, similarly, are benevolent if they are properly tended and served. The constraints of religion, experienced most acutely when ancestors act in a punitive manner, are the counterpart of the constraints of family life experienced whenever parents impose their will. In doing this they are bound to thwart their children and this is enough to arouse suspicions that they are angry, even if they seem to show no signs of this. At bottom, it is the same set of norms operating in the two spheres. Indeed, these spheres overlap for, as we have seen, the powers and status of parents are backed by the sanctions of the ancestor cult.

Here it is worth repeating that the normal personal relationships of parents and children are warm and friendly. Fathers and sons trust and support one another at the same time that they carefully observe the restrictions proper to their relationship as members of successive generations. This too is reflected in the worship of the ancestors. The prayers offered at sacrifices are never abject. They explain the circumstances, perhaps express contrition, but end in phrases which, for all their persuasive and appeasing form, imply that the giver of the sacrifice expects a benevolent return. And this is the root of the attitude and belief that, in the last resort, whatever the ancestors decree is just.

CHAPTER IX

FATE IN RELATION TO THE SOCIAL STRUCTURE

WE seem to have wandered far from the contrast between Oedipus and Job with which we began. Precisely in what sense are our paradigms applicable to the religious institutions of the Tallensi? Faced with this question Frazer would have looked for connexions in common human experiences and mental processes. As I remarked at the outset, I think he was right in principle but was misled by the premisses which he took over from the science of his day. The descriptive parallels between Tale beliefs and our paradigms are patent, and Frazer would have given his attention to them rather than to the underlying meanings that primarily interest us.

Frazer derived ancestor-worship from a belief in the immortality of the soul, coupled with a fear of the dead, which he thought was virtually instinctive among mankind.[1] Such an explanation would be

---

[1] This is a typical Frazerian hypothesis. It is expounded at great and sesquipedalian length in *The Belief in Immortality* (1913); see especially vol. I, pp. 23 ff., vol. II, pp. 57 ff. It is also introduced in other contexts, e.g. *Totemism and Exogamy* (1910), vol. IV, p. 32.

a ludicrous oversimplification for the Tallensi, or any other West-African people. The Tallensi have an ancestor cult not because they fear the dead—for they do not, in fact, do so—nor because they believe in the immortality of the soul—for they have no such notion—but because their social structure demands it. To put it in other words, they have a complex and elaborate body of ritual beliefs and practices for perpetuating and regulating the significance of the dead in the lives of their descendants. They worship their ancestors because ancestry, and more particularly parenthood, is the critical and irreducible determinant of their whole social structure. Not fear, ignorance or superstition but the moral bonds of the filio-parental relationship are the springs of Tale ancestor-worship. The significant parallels with Oedipus and Job lie in this.

We have seen that Tale jural and ritual concepts distinguish with precision a number of elements in the social and individual constitution of a person by reference to the different domains of social structure in which they are effective. We have noted that the mere fact of being born alive and remaining alive is the primary element. This receives a specific ritual imprimatur in the institution of the spirit guardian. The spirit guardian serves both to identify and to give value to the fact of individual life and to show how it depends on parental care. It is because one owes one's life to one's parents, Tallensi say, that one has irrevocable and absolute bonds with them.[1] First there are the affective and moral bonds which Tallensi derive from the relationship of upbringing. Parental discipline, authority, affection and care create reciprocal dependence, obedience, and respectful love on the part of the children. Then there is the jural component of status in one's lineage and locus in the web of kinship, acquired by birth, through one's parents, and forming an element in the continuity of the social structure through time. The ritual imprimatur for this is the conception of the ancestors as sovereign and eternal, mirroring the total system of kinship and descent which is seen as an everlasting and fixed framework for the individual's social existence. Lastly there are the bonds created by the succession of generations. Sons must succeed fathers and daughters mothers in the passage of the generations. This is jurally expressed in the facts of inheritance and succession and ritually demonstrated in the worship of the spirits of the dead parents.

In this context the critical fact is that the individual has no choice. Submission to his ancestors is symbolic of his encapsulation in a social order which permits of no voluntary alteration of his status and social capacities. It is the common interest, the collective purposes that prevail.

We can see that an individual who was incurably

[1] Cf. what was said of Job, pp. 17–18 above.

impeded from fitting into the social structure would be an anomaly. Hence the great importance of giving specific ritual recognition to the individuality of each life-history. It acknowledges the need for the realities of life to be accommodated to the fixity of structural norms; and it is easy to see how notions of luck, chance, destiny and even, in a more sophisticated idiom, election, could be used to reconcile the determinism of jural and ritual status imposed by the social structure with the variability and unpredictability of the individual life-cycle. If we imagine a graph of a person's life among the Tallensi, one axis would stand for his movement into and through the social structure, the other for his personal development, the origin being the fact of his being born alive of particular parents.

This is where Oedipal concepts come into evidence. They recognize forces in social and personal development that cannot be changed or regulated by society. The Tale notion of Prenatal Destiny designates what, in more abstract language, could best be described as an innate disposition that can be realized either for good or for ill. The Tallensi themselves do not, of course, have the cultural resources for analysing their religious symbolism in this a form. Indeed, if they were able to do so the symbols would be denuded of their affective and expressive force. It is only the outside investigator, viewing the symbolism in relation to the other religious institutions of those who live by them, and in its context of social structure, who can perceive its abstract meaning.

What strikes us then is the criteria by which a person's evil Prenatal Destiny is diagnosed. Proof that it is working itself out in an evil way is the victim's irremediable but involuntary failure to fulfil the roles and achieve the performance regarded as normal for his status in the social structure. It would not be going too far to say that the Tallensi define a person as being afflicted by an evil Prenatal Destiny if he turns out to be incapable of being or remaining incorporated in the social structure. If, on the other hand, he gains and holds his due place in it, this is credited to his Good Destiny.

Why, then, is the victim of an evil Prenatal Destiny dissociated from the social structure? Tale doctrine and ritual usage imply that it is because he has, from the moment of birth, rejected society, preferring death to incorporation in the network of fundamental family and kinship relations and turning his back on the basic moral norms. This is not a conscious or deliberate rejection, since the sufferer is not aware of his predisposition until he learns of it through divination. From the point of view of society, as expressed in Tale doctrine, the fault lies in his inescapable, inborn wishes. But from the sufferer's point of view, as shown in his attitudes and conduct, his condition is forced upon him by society. He sees himself as implicitly disowned by his kin and his ancestors, since all the resources of social organization, therapeutic skill, ritual, and parental devotion have failed to open a way to social normality for him. He is justified in this because the sovereign authority over his life so obviously resides in society and because the notion of Prenatal Destiny is a last ditch defence. Those responsible for his well-being only fall back on it, with the sanction of a diviner's findings, when appeals to the ancestors to save him have come to nought. What is symbolized in the notion of evil Prenatal Destiny is, therefore, a failure in the relationship of belonging to society, which, for the Tallensi, means family, lineage and kin. In developmental terms this means a failure in the primary relationships of parents and children, since it is through these relationships that the individual is fitted into society and the norms and the demands of society are implanted in him.

These structural considerations suggest a number of parallels in the story of Oedipus. His fate is evil; it enters into his life at the very beginning through his being rejected by his parents when they cast him away. He survives only because he is accepted by substitute parents, but he becomes an outcast again when his fate catches up with him. He is finally overwhelmed by his fate because he unknowingly violates the basic norms of the filial relationship. His tragedy can be described as that of a man blindly seeking to achieve his legitimate place in society, first as son, then as husband, father and citizen against the unconscious opposition of an inborn urge to avenge himself by repudiating his parents, his spouse, and his children. When, in the end, he succumbs to this fate he shows his revulsion against himself by mutilating his own eyes and so blotting out his relationship with his kin and his society. Nor is he ever accepted back into society. He dies in exile, almost like a ghost departing from this world rather than like an ordinary man.

We must remember, however, that the notion of Prenatal Destiny is not merely a label for a class of persons definable in structural terms. It is a religious concept, associated with ritual procedures for disposing, by symbolic 'displacement, of the emotional and moral tensions generated in the structural antinomies in which the fated individual finds himself. We have seen how it serves to exonerate both society and the sufferer by fixing ultimate responsibility on the ancestors and on a pre-natal, that is pre-social, event. Thus the onus of the rejection is shifted on to the supernatural plane and the individual's feelings of helplessness and depression are made tolerable. In the case of Oedipus, too, the onus of guilt falls on fate. Even his father and mother are victims of this hereditary determinism. Where the Oedipus story diverges most strikingly from the simpler Tale pattern is in the place assigned to human will. Laius and Jocasta thought they could thwart Fate by casting away their child. They failed; and the Tallensi would understand this, for they do not believe that hostile supernatural forces can be averted by human prudence. Only ritual measures can, in their scheme of thought, defend them against supernatural threats.

The reason lies in the Tale concept of mystical causation mentioned earlier in this essay. Its effect is seen in the beliefs and practices related to the process by which the innate potentiality of Destiny is turned to beneficial ends. The evidence for its beneficence is demonstrated capacity to achieve the economic, jural and social goals that are normal for a person's age, sex and status. But continued beneficence is only ensured if particular (ideally paternal) ancestors accept the supernatural responsibility for his Destiny. We can readily see that this is the expression, in religious symbols and sanctions, of the ideal of the parents (particularly the father) as beings who accept their child in order to care for him throughout his life. Since Destiny ancestors are the agents of the collective ancestors, their role is also the symbolic equivalent of incorporating him into the political and jural domain of the social structure in his character as a person with a unique life-cycle. Consequently, when a man submits to his ancestors he is accepting his dependence on his parents, particularly his father and, *a fortiori*, his incorporation

in society. This is an absolute—that is, super-
naturally sanctioned—relationship, in which the duty
to abide by the basic moral axioms of society is
appropriated by each person as a supreme value. It
is the very opposite condition to that of a supposed
victim of evil Prenatal Destiny. In the abstract
terms we have been using, we would say that har-
nessing the individual's inborn potentialities to the
needs and values of society prevents them from
becoming destructive and turns them into capacities
for productive social development and normal life
in society.

To put the argument in a slightly different way,
if parents fail in their task of upbringing, the latent
hostility of their children in their relations with
them and sentiments towards them gets the upper
hand—or at least it is deemed to do so—and eventually destroys the bonds between them. Evil Prenatal Destiny conceptualizes this experience. On
the other hand, if parents succeed in this task, it
shows that they have used the powers and authority
vested in them by society with benevolence—in
religious terms, with the blessings of the ancestors.
Conversely, it also shows that their children have
responded to parental discipline, care and affection
with growth to adulthood. This means that trustful
acquiescence towards their parents has been more
powerful than latent antagonism. The notion of the
Good Destiny conceptualizes this experience and

gives sanction and value to it as a lasting moral force in the individual's life. This is where Tale beliefs are quite unlike the story of Oedipus. For him there was no way of changing his evil fate into a beneficent destiny. But it is reminiscent of Job.

Figuratively speaking, therefore, we might say that an Oedipal predisposition is in this way transformed into a Jobian fulfilment. The drama of Job's life springs from the circumstance that he is chosen by his god in order to put his fidelity to test. It is comparable to the way Destiny ancestors choose their ward among the Tallensi and continually try his faith by making demands on him. This is one indication among many that Job is never disowned, avowedly or implicitly, by either his fellows or his god. The tribulations he endures are of a quite different order from the catastrophes brought on Oedipus by irrevocable fate. They can, as I suggested at the beginning, well be compared to a severe but just form of paternal correction, and that is why they are not tragic like those of Oedipus but simply pathetic though on a cosmic scale. They are, in fact, part of the total texture of a relationship with his fellows and his god in which he is cherished, despite appearances to the contrary, and which he never turns away from. Such a relationship is essential for God, the superior, to be in a position to chastize Job, and for Job, the inferior, to be in a position to defend himself by righteous conduct and argument. It is true that Job at first feels himself estranged from his fellows and persecuted unjustly by God. This is because he mistakes his status and believes himself entitled to recognition and reward in terms of his own standards of virtue and right. Tallensi would not fall into this error in relation to their ancestors.

Job's salvation comes when he recognizes his god's omnipotence as a phenomenon beyond human questioning. He perceives that submission to his god must be absolute, whether or not it corresponds to norms of righteous conduct among men. This is submission in the attitude of filial humility and faith towards all-powerful parents. In this relationship it is possible, and indeed inevitable, for the inferior to accept everything willed for him by his superior, whether it turns out to his advantage or not, as an act of justice. In Job's case it makes his tribulations appear as the means by which he was taught a true understanding of the nature of his dependence on God and of the services befitting to this relationship. It is appropriate that he is in the end restored not only to God's favour,[1] but to health, status and rank. The Tallensi would understand this story very well by analogy with their ancestor cult; for Oedipus, such a road back to normality does not exist.

[1] We remember how, at the end of the drama, God declares '...for him will I accept...' (Job xlii. 8).

75

CHAPTER X

RECAPITULATION

To recapitulate, the notion of evil Prenatal Destiny among the Tallensi serves to identify the fact of irremediable failure in the development of the individual to full social capacity. More than that, it gives symbolic expression to the implicit structural meaning of such failure as an indication of abortive filio-parental relationships. The possibility of these relationships going wrong is a threat to fundamental moral and affective ties and sentiments. This is neutralized by ritual procedures based on the belief that evil Prenatal Destiny is in the last resort susceptible of control by the ancestors if they so will it. Thus the ill-fated are by implication those unfortunate people who are felt to be rejected by the parental institutions of society symbolized in the ancestor figures. The hostile component in the filio-parental relationship comes to the fore, and is given symbolic expression in the image of evil Prenatal Destiny which finally destroys its victim.

The notion of Good Destiny, on the other hand, symbolically identifies the fact of successful individual development along the road to full incorporation in society. It serves to make this fact comprehensible and to set a seal of religious value on it as implicitly significant of normal and successful filio-parental relationships. The symbolism utilized is the notion that Destiny operates in this way if it is absorbed and sanctioned by the ancestors. It thus accounts for the rewards that witness to successful development, and provides a basis for ritual procedures to neutralize the demoralizing effects, on fundamental moral and affective ties and sentiments, of the hazards that accompany each person's progress through life. The well-fated are by implication those fortunate enough to be accepted by the parental institutions symbolized in the cult of the ancestors and endowed with the ability to maintain relationships of mutual trust and support with them. This means that the hostile component in the filio-parental relationship is overcome in the attribution of a predominantly benevolent character to the ancestors. In this context the punitive aspect of the ancestor figures has a disciplinary not a destructive function. It is the instrument of their justice and a measure of their sovereignty paralleling, on the religious plane, the usages and forms of family government we have previously described. It helps to drain away individual feelings of anxiety and guilt by canalizing them into customary rituals of placation and expiation; and these are effective simply because the ancestors are believed not only to exact punishment for wrong conduct but also

77

to behave justly and benevolently in the long run.

What can we learn from this limited inquiry? Frazer's own work is a warning against drawing facile generalizations from parallels between the customs and beliefs of widely different societies. However, my aim in this essay has not been to find parallels but to elicit basic common elements in the religious conceptions I have described. And one common element is patent. All the concepts and beliefs we have examined are religious extrapolations of the experiences generated in the relationships between parents and children in societies with a social organization based on kinship and descent. They are magnified and disguised extrapolations; and their effect is to endow the critical components of filio-parental relationships with an external reality and representation that belongs to the whole society and not to the realm of individual thought and fantasy. The religious conceptions of the Tallensi show us this process in a direct form. We can uncover the roots of these beliefs in the family system and observe how their branches spread through the entire social structure. We can see how they bind the internal domain of the family, where children are reared, to the external domain of political society, where they eventually run their life-course; and we can see why parenthood, on the one hand, and the sovereignty of society, on the other, are invested with sacredness.

Oedipus and Job dramatize the basic elements of this type of religious system. They, too, are reflexions, partly exact, partly distorted, of family and kinship institutions. If they appeal more to our imagination and emotions than do the unsophisticated facts of Tale religion, this is because they deck out the bare bones of belief and concept in the rich panoply of the ethical thought and metaphysical doctrines of literate cultures. The core of fundamental beliefs and attitudes is the same.

Here, then, are the areas of common human experience to which our data must be referred. Ever since Freud's bold speculations in *Totem and Taboo* and Durkheim's great work on *The Elementary Forms of the Religious Life*, anthropologists have known that the springs of religion and ritual lie in kinship and social organization. What I have tried to do has been to relate particular religious conceptions to the significance, for the society, of the process of taking its individual members into itself. Considered merely as superstition, beliefs in Fate and the Ancestors (or Job's God) seem to be antithetical. The first is amoral, the second is supremely moral. In fact, we have seen that in West African religions they are not opposed but rather supplement each other. For the Tallensi, at any rate, they can be described as supplementary conceptual moments in a religious apparatus for dealing with the commitments created for society collectively and for its members severally by the passage of the individual into and through society.[1] They reconcile the two main alternatives in the hazardous progress of the individual from the state of unchecked dependence, as an infant at the mother's breast, to that of constrained independence, as an adult and citizen. It is a law of nature that some people must fail in the whole or in parts of the task of becoming and remaining social persons. The predicament this gives rise to is interpreted, given moral value, and brought under control in the interests of society and of the individual, by means of the beliefs and rituals focused in the notion of Predestiny, or Oedipal Fate. Most people will succeed; but they can do so only by coming to terms with unforeseeable hazards and precarious rewards. To give meaning and absolute moral value to this experience the Tallensi invoke personified supernatural figures cast in the mould of glorified parents who intervene justly in the life of the individual and of society. The image of the Good Destiny in which these ideas are focused is, in essentials, a simple version of Job's God.

In the ultimate sense, perhaps, the concept of Predestiny may be taken to designate tendencies that originate in organic sources and in the earliest experiences of infantile dependence. It is of pro-

[1] Cf. Goody, Jack (ed.), *The Developmental Cycle in Domestic Groups*, Cambridge Papers in Social Anthropology, No. 1 (1958), for the analysis of other aspects of this problem.

found interest that these tendencies appear to be intuitively recognized in many societies and are deemed to manifest themselves in unwitting resistance to the normal relationships of parenthood. Ancestor- or deity-worship, on the other hand, presupposes the triumph of parenthood. It recognizes the paramountcy of the moral norms emanating from society as a whole over the dangerous egotism of childhood.

This essay is an expansion of the Frazer Lecture for 1956 delivered at the University of Glasgow on 28 November 1957 under the title of 'The Idea of Destiny in West African Religions'. I am indebted to the Ford Foundation (Behavioral Sciences Division) for a grant for research assistance in preparing it for publication and to Dr Christopher Scott and Dr Lucy Mair for helpful criticism.

Date Due

THREE DAY			
MY 24 '67			
OC 6 '69			
OC 30 '82			
AP 27 '84			
NO 17 '97			
DEC 16 '00			
Demco 293-5			

CPSIA information can be obtained
at www.ICGtesting.com
Printed in the USA
BVHW052314130223
658471BV00002B/49